MW00535063

VIVA —LA— PIZZA!

VIVA LA PIZZA!

THE ART OF THE PIZZA BOX

▲ MELVILLE HOUSE
BROOKLYN · LONDON

Scott Wiener

VIVA LA PIZZA!

Copyright © 2013 by Scott Wiener

First Melville House printing: November 2013

Melville House Publishing   8 Blackstock Mews
            145 Plymouth Street   and Islington
            Brooklyn, NY 11201   London N4 2BT

mhpbooks.com   facebook.com/mhpbooks   @melvillehouse

ISBN: 978-1-61219-307-6

Book design by Christopher King

Printed in the United States of America
1 3 5 7 9 10 8 6 4 2

A catalog record for this title is available
from the Library of Congress.

Contents

THE ART OF THE PIZZA BOX

INTRODUCTION
A BRIEF HISTORY OF THE PIZZA BOX

The story of the pizza box is also the story of pizza, which began its existence as a humble street food in southern Italy. As far back as the sixteenth century, leftover dough was placed in bread ovens as a tool to cool down the hearth; the dough absorbed heat, and leftover produce or pork fat was placed on top to prevent it from inflating due to steam buildup. The resulting pies were sold from the bakery counter or on the street, sometimes by mobile vendors who distributed pizza in a *stufa*, a metal vessel used as a warmer that was a predecessor to the modern pizza box. Concepts like pizza by the slice and home delivery have their roots in the hectic port city of Naples, a town whose low position in Italy's cultural hierarchy kept it isolated from the rest of the country. Italians did their best to avoid Naples and anything Neapolitan, so pizza never spread up the boot.

Pizza's first expansion out of southern Italy occurred in the late nineteenth century, when political and economic factors drove impoverished citizens to find work in the growing industrial sector of the United States. Dozens of "Little Italys" developed in major cities, including Trenton, New Haven, Providence, St. Louis, Chicago, San Francisco, Boston, Philadelphia, and New York. Pizza was then introduced to the greater Italian diaspora as a snack food, but since Italian neighborhoods were often quite small, it never needed to travel far enough to necessitate a box. Cheap newsprint provided pizza's only packaging at the time, and it remained this way for the first half of the twentieth century.

Exposure to Italian food and culture later inspired droves of American GIs to bring the dish back home after World War II. It was essentially the first time that non-Italians were eating pizza, and it resulted in a seismic shift in global pizza consumption that we're still feeling today.

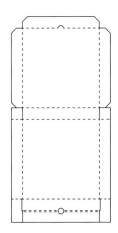

▲ A Walker-style blank as it is delivered to pizzerias

▲ The original corrugated Domino's Pizza box, designed by the Triad company to improve stability and insulation

Once the label of "ethnic cuisine" was removed, American interest in pizza grew exponentially, and soon American pizza took its own path. Ingredient availability and social factors led to regional variations across the country. The dry heat of New York's coal ovens produced thin, beautifully charred pizzas; avoidance of expensive mozzarella cheese led to tomato pies in Trenton and Philadelphia; and the Midwestern appetite paved the way for the development of the deep-dish pizza in 1940s Chicago.

Soon pizza was everywhere, and everyone was eating it. Moreover, everybody was taking it to go. Paperboard bakery boxes were an early mode of American pizza transportation. Some boxes had pre-glued corners that flattened down for shipping and easily popped into place for use. But the high cost of producing pre-glued boxes pushed self-locking paperboard to the forefront. These boxes shipped as a stack of cut and scored blanks whose front and back walls easily locked into adjacent sidewall slots.

The major problem with these paperboard or "clay" boxes is that they aren't very sturdy. Unlike their intended cargo of dry cookies and cake, steaming hot pizza has a tendency to weaken a box from the inside. Even empty clay boxes were a hazard in busy pizzerias; their instability threatened spontaneous

▶ Big Mama's & Papa's Pizzeria in Los Angeles offers a fifty-four-inch square pizza that is packaged in the world's largest commercially available pizza box. The pizza is so large that a custom extension is attached to the oven for added space and support. It feeds fifty to seventy people and must be delivered on a roof-mounted car rack because it can't fit inside any standard automobile. The pizza costs $218 (with tax), plus $15 per topping, and delivery starts at $30 but escalates with distance. At least the box is "free."

avalanches. The solution came at the request of a growing pizza chain called Domino's Pizza, whose founder, Tom Monaghan, enlisted a corrugated box company called Triad to solve the problem. In 1966, after some serious tinkering, a box was finally constructed to suit the needs of what was then only a four-store chain. As a better insulator and a sturdier structure, the corrugated container initiated a new era in the history of the pizza box.

Large pizza operators eventually realized the marketing potential of their box tops and started printing their names and logos in the 1960s. Mom-and-pop pizzerias caught on more than a decade later with their own short-run semi-custom boxes. Pizzerias had their names printed alongside any combination of generic images (the boot of Italy, a mustachioed chef, Italian flags). It wasn't until the late 1990s that four-color process printing turned pizza boxes into art. Designs were broken down into cyan, magenta, yellow, and black components, and printed one color at a time as small dots with flexographic printing machines. Box companies wanted to show off their full capabilities and began courting customers to submit art. Roma Foods, a distributor in the northeast, dove in headfirst with a series of full-color designs starting around 1995 (see page 60), and others quickly followed.

As beautiful as they may have been, full-color prints didn't catch on with American pizzerias due to their high costs. The trend overseas is entirely different, particularly in pizza's birthplace of Naples. According to the most prolific pizza box artist, Luca Ciancio, Italian box art is superior to that of all other countries because of a greater respect for the product within. On a mechanical level, the printed box industry in Italy is much younger than that in America, and newer machines allow for more accurate reproductions of complex designs.

Unlike these advancements in pizza box art, little has changed with box technology. The corrugated pizza box has been a simple and cost-effective solution since the 1970s, yet hundreds of inventors have attempted to improve upon it. In 1991, a patent was filed for a box that breaks down into serving plates. A few

HOW ARE PIZZA BOXES MADE?

Pizza box production typically does not impact American forests. Quality lumber is more useful for building construction than it is in the packaging industry, which opts for secondary sources like twigs and small scraps. A good amount of raw material also comes from OCC, or Old Corrugated Cartons, which make up the recycled content of paper-based packaging like pizza boxes. This material can be processed five times before it gets filtered out of the supply stream.

All material gets pulped and cured into rolls of liner, which form the individual layers of a corrugated sheet. The outer liner gets glued to a fluted medium before an inner liner is attached to the opposite side of the medium. All three sections are bonded with an adhesive made from starch and water, most of which is recycled from other uses within the box plant. The finished corrugated sheet then gets printed with flexographic plates and cut with a curved die. Scraps of discarded corrugated board get reintroduced into the system to be used in the next pulping phase.

The finished stack of blanks is packed and shipped to its destination, likely a pizzeria or distribution center. Once inside a pizzeria, boxes are folded and stacked for use at the beginning of every shift before being filled and delivered to the customer. Once used, the box is broken down by the customer and then set out for recycling, potentially to be transformed into another pizza box.

chains even auditioned boxes that could fit a second pizza stacked on top of the first. Several circular pizza containers were patented in the 1990s, theoretically better suited for transporting likewise circular pizzas. Then there were boxes with built-in support systems to protect the container and the pizza from each other. One of the more fascinating patents is called "Disposable Pizza-Blotting Composite and Box Assembly," poised to solve the problem of overly greasy pizza with a self-blotting lid. Another favorite is the "Level-Indicating Pizza Box," a patent filed by J. Gus Prokopis in 1998. The box has a built-in spirit level so the user can be sure they're carrying their pizza correctly. All interesting solutions for problems the market doesn't deem necessary to fix.

Such innovations add cost for the pizzeria, so none of these box designs

What does a box cost an
independent pizzeria?

$0.20	corrugated circle (16 inches)
$0.08	paper pizza bag (16 inches)
$0.12	generic clay box (12 inches)
$0.15	customized clay box (12 inches)
$0.33	generic corrugated box (16 inches)
$0.40	customized corrugated box (16 inches)
$0.62	automatic box (16 inches)
$0.01	Package Saver (doll-house table, sold in packs of 100)
$0.95	La Hacienda fiftieth-anniversary box (page 72)
$0.99	Picasso's Pizza Biondo box (pages 46–47)

have yet to become as ubiquitous as the standard corrugated folder. Since boxes are an invisible cost to customers, most pizzerias don't see the benefit of investing. Real buying power remains with the chains and their edict to cut pennies. Such cost cutting has had a dramatic impact on box designs, including an arms race of sorts in the late 1980s to build a sturdy box using less raw material. Kenneth J. Zion and Richard H. Johnson invented the first octagonal pizza box for Stone Container Corporation in 1987. It was a victory that inspired a flood of structural innovation, resulting in Anthony Deiger's 1990 patent "Container with Improved Retention Properties and Improved Corner Structures." The improved corner structure, called a wedge-lock, solved structural issues with prior designs. It was this wedge-lock that became an integral element in the 1996 design by Nicholas A. Philips and Walter D. Keefe, Jr., called "Single-Piece Food Package." The pizza box industry refers to it as the D-cut because it looks like a capital D when turned sideways.

Individual operators are typically unenthusiastic about making big changes to their box. Old-schoolers believe that if they give people what they're used to, they won't lose customers. Box manufacturers have trouble convincing clients to try something different, even if it will give them a marketing advantage or save a few pennies. Most pizzerias are so used to the standard corrugation known as "B flute" that they refuse to switch to the thinner and less expensive E-flute substrate, even though it would save space and money. As pizza is about tradition, some changes seem inadvisable to operators. And so we are left with a box that looks more or less the same as pizza's first delivery containers invented six decades ago.

WHY PIZZA BOXES?

I was traveling through Israel in January 2008 when I spotted a brightly colored yellow pizza box. Up until this moment, I had known pizza boxes only as soft white paperboard printed with faded red ink. Seeing so much color on a pizza box took me by surprise. I took a photo and moved on—but something about the box stayed with me, because I was soon noticing other interesting boxes everywhere I went.

I don't remember the first box I saved, but a collection was definitely starting to amass just months after that first spotting. I was spending lots of time in pizzerias because I had just launched a business called Scott's Pizza Tours, in which I and a team of dedicated pizza enthusiasts lead excursions to great pizzerias in New York City. I was also part of a crew tasked with visiting more than three hundred pizzerias in New Jersey for the state's largest newspaper, *The Star-Ledger*. Our reviews appeared weekly, a constant reminder that my life was becoming more pizza-centric. My roommates loved my work because it meant

The world's first pizza box wasn't a box at all. A *stufa* is a metal vessel that dates back to the eighteenth century. It was used to carry fresh pizzas around the streets of Naples. The cylindrical warmer's copper exterior prevents the carrier from being burned—especially important in that the *stufa* was often balanced on the carrier's head. Multiple pizzas could be folded in half to protect their toppings, almost like calzones, and stacked inside for safe transport. The *stufa* was then covered with a pointed lid so steam could escape through three small vents about halfway toward the peak, with each vent covered to protect the contents of the container.

This *stufa* demonstrates pizza's inherent portability and reminds us that even though pizza may taste best when eaten fresh from the oven, its most basic requirements are to be hot and convenient. No longer in use, the *stufa* remains a display piece in many Neapolitan pizzerias.

a steady flow of leftover slices—and those slices came in boxes. Most boxes were mundane, so I saved only those I thought unique enough to deserve space in a tiny Brooklyn apartment.

The collection kicked into high gear as I shared my fascination with my pizza tour customers, many of whom hail from faraway lands. Packages soon poured in from France, Hungary, Turkey, and the Netherlands. They were too interesting to keep to myself, so I decided to organize a small exhibition at a Greenwich Village travel agency in 2010. We had about twenty boxes from a dozen different countries. Some were generic and others were customized for particular pizzerias, but each told a story about its culture of origin.

More boxes came in after the show. A friend scored beauties from Switzerland, Ecuador, Liechtenstein, and Cuba thanks to her perfection of the phrase "Can I please have a box without the pizza?" in all appropriate languages. I once met up with a guy on a Manhattan street corner so he could hand off an incredible box he'd found in New Zealand. A pizzeria operator in Austria sends me new boxes every few months in exchange for maximum-strength eye drops he can't get back home.

I've since planned vacations around visits to pizza box manufacturers in New York, Boston, Tampa, and even Italy. Late-night phone calls with pizza box designers in Japan and India have shed light on the latest innovations in the industry. I've pulled boxes out of garbage cans in Sicily, looted booths at pizza industry tradeshows, and even made a few shameful purchases on eBay. Every curbside recycling pile holds potential for discovery, and every film or TV show becomes more interesting the moment a pizza box enters the frame.

As I built my collection, it occurred to me that pizza box art might be the most underappreciated medium of our time. Some generic images have been printed tens of millions of times. Even some of the world's greatest works of art haven't been produced at these numbers. When I finally started connecting with the artists who created the box art, it became clear that these images were by far their best-known works—and were works they were proud of.

This book is an opportunity to honor the efforts of these unsung artists and analyze the images they've created while also tracing the development of the medium itself. We'll see some of the most beautiful pizza boxes from around the world as well as the most obscure. Some will look familiar and others barely look like pizza boxes, but I assure you they are all real and are, I believe, art.

▲ The generic stock box used by my local pizzeria while I was growing up in suburban New Jersey

KEY TERMS

AUTOMATIC BOX: The automatic box is the missing link of pizza containers because it represents the evolutionary step between boxes used in bakeries and those used in pizzerias. In an automatic box, all four corners are pre-glued for quick setup. Regardless of its ease of use, this is the weakest of all box structures.

Production cost for the automatic box is much higher than for self-locking blanks because of the pre-gluing in manufacturing. Automatic pizza boxes can still be found in Ohio, where the design likely originated.

BLANK: A finished single sheet of fiberboard that includes all perforations and scoring necessary for construction of the final box (i.e., a pre-folded pizza box).

CARDBOARD: A single layer of compressed fiber used for shipping and packaging. Typically used for shoeboxes, cereal boxes, toilet paper rolls, and thin pizza boxes. Not to be confused with corrugated board.

CHICAGO FOLDER: As indicated by its name, this box originated in the Windy City. The three walls fold at right angles to the base but aren't secure until the two trapezoidal ears located on the lid's upper corners are wedged into the openings on either side of the base, effectively locking the entire unit together.

This unique pattern offers an ideal container for Chicago's deep-dish pizzas because all four walls collapse once the box is opened, making it much easier to serve thick deep-dish pizza than would be possible with locked-base boxes. This type uses more paper than the standard boxes because its blank is wider, leaving excess portions of corrugated substrate.

CLAY: A term for single-layer coated cardboard pizza boxes. These are sometimes referred to as "paperboard" or "chipboard" if they lack a coating.

CONVERSION: The process of printing onto a blank substrate.

CORNER-CUT: The great contradiction of transporting a circular pizza inside a square box is tackled head-on by this revolutionary structure. The sidewalls fold into place along scored lines, as they do with standard boxes, but angled corners make all the difference. These corners pop inward, holding in place only after the front-lid flap is anchored inside the base's front wall. The corners give this box more strength than square boxes, resulting in cleaner stacking and tighter pizza carriage. It's also much easier to fold than other boxes, so fewer man-hours are required.

The corner-cut design uses 7 percent less paper than standard boxes, significantly lowering its production cost. It was first introduced to the pizza industry by Stone Container Corporation in the late 1980s (Octagonal Carton for Pizza Pies or the Like, by Zion et al.; patent #4,765,534) and modified by An- thony J. Deiger shortly thereafter (patent #4,919,326). A version by Nicholas A. Philips et al. for Weyerhaeuser Company (patent #5,702,054) is currently in use by Domino's.

CORRUGATION: The process of combining a flat outer liner with a fluted medium. Creates significantly more structural integrity than single-layer cardboard boxes.

CUSTOM PRINT: An image designed specifically for a particular customer (i.e., a pizzeria). May be composed of stock images or completely unique.

DIE CUTTER: A specialized tool used to cut, perforate, and score a substrate. This determines the structure and folding style of a box.

DLK: Short for "double-lined kraft." Refers to scraps cut from freshly die-cut boxes that are then re-bailed for use in the recycled content stream.

EURO LOCK: Although it isn't common in the United States, this pattern is ubiquitous across Europe. Two tabs at the lower ends of the side panels pop through corresponding openings in the front wall, holding in place like the clasp on a shipping envelope.

European boxes are usually made with a much thinner fluting than their American counterparts. The resulting box works well for light Italian pizzas but lacks the strength and stability required by thicker, heavier American pizzas. Shorter flutes also provide a more precise surface for printing.

FILL IN: An unclear print caused by a soft printing plate, dust buildup, or low ink pH.

FLASH: An accidental colorless gap between two printed areas, caused by registration errors and avoided by trapping.

FLEXOGRAPHY (FLEXO): The most common method of printing on corrugated substrates. Uses a curved rubber relief plate to transfer images onto substrate.

FLUTE: The waved inner medium of a corrugated sheet used to give it strength. Common flute sizes for pizza boxes are B and E, each of which refers to a different frequency of waves per linear foot.

HALFTONE: A printing technique used to diffuse ink into a spectrum of shades by decreasing resolution. Useful in gradients and creating optical illusions of lighter shades of a particular color.

HALO: An unintentional border surrounding printed sections due to excessive plate pressure.

HOLDING LINE: A border line around an image that serves to cover for registration issues during printing. Also known as a "keyline."

KNOCKOUT: A design technique in which different colors are positioned next to one another rather than overlapping.

KRAFT: A type of paper produced by a chemical pulping process, usually dark brown in color.

LINER: Refers to the inner and outer layers of corrugated board, usually white or brown in color and made of either recycled or virgin paper.

B FLUTE

154 +/− 10 flutes per linear meter (3.2mm thick)

E FLUTE

295 +/− 13 flutes per linear meter (1.6mm thick)

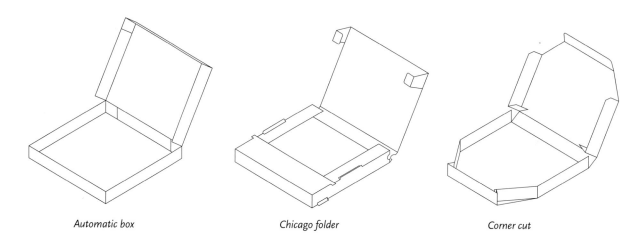

Automatic box   *Chicago folder*   *Corner cut*

MEDIUM: The fluted inner layer of a corrugated box responsible for increased stability, especially over that of clay boxes.

OCC: Short for "Old Corrugated Cartons." Used as raw material for recycled content of pizza boxes.

OVERPRINTING: The technique of printing a darker ink directly over a lighter ink to avoid visual problems caused by registration issues.

PAPERBOARD: Refers to any compressed paper-based material. Also known as clay, cardboard, or chipboard.

PREPRINT: The method by which the outer liner is printed before being combined with the inner medium to create a corrugated board. Often used with digital photo-quality printing on advertising boxes.

PRINTING PLATE: A relief composed of raised elements to be printed on a substrate. A different plate is used for each color being imprinted.

PROCESS PRINTING: The method of printing complex full-color images by separating design into four colors: cyan, magenta, yellow, and black (CMYK).

REGISTRATION: The alignment of multiple color printing plates.

SEMI-CUSTOM: A type of graphic design containing a mixture of stock images and pizzeria-specific information.

SPECTRODENSITOMETER: A device used by a printer to check color accuracy.

SPOT PRINTING: The method of printing simple colors in solid blocks of ink, similar to stamping.

STOCK BOX: An image designed for use by multiple pizzerias. Sold to pizzerias by box manufacturers and food distributors. A less expensive alternative to custom prints.

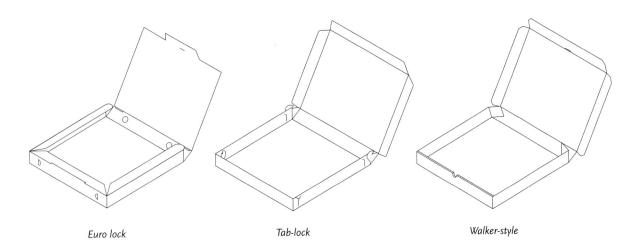

Euro lock · *Tab-lock* · *Walker-style*

STOCK IMAGE: A royalty-free graphic featured on stock and semi-custom boxes.

SUBSTRATE: The material to be printed.

TAB-LOCK: Early pizza boxes utilized this pattern, which is based on that of deeper bakery boxes. To assemble, simply crease along the score marks and insert all four hooked tabs into their corresponding slots. The base's walls lock together, but the box often requires a package saver (see page 109) for necessary support when stacking additional pizzas boxes.

The lack of stability renders this box type inferior for packaging whole pies but useful for take-out slices.

TRAPPING: The intentional extension of the image outline to compensate for registration problems during conversion. Used in spot printing but not with process printing.

WALKER-STYLE: This is the most popular pizza-box structure in the United States. To construct the box, simply fold in the perforated sidewalls and fold the end tabs inward at right angles. Next, flip the front wall over the tabs and click it into place through two notches at the base of the front wall. This forms a sturdy structure into which the lid's three walls are closed.

The origin of the name Walker may be an inaccurate reference to an early rollover locking mechanism called the Folding Tray, patented by Elmer L. Winkler in 1951 (patent #2,563,145). Some companies refer to it as Michigan Style, likely after its early adoption by Michigan-based pizzerias in the 1970s.

WASHBOARD EFFECT: A printing flaw resulting in visible ink stripes along the flutes of a corrugated board as a result of high printing plate pressure.

WHITETOP: The bleached kraft liner usually used as the outer surface of pizza boxes for cleaner printing.

CLASSIC AMERICAN

▲ This New Jersey pizzeria uses a popular map of Italy.

▲ Margherita Pizza in Jamaica, Queens, uses a familiar map of Italy, likely printed with an older plate, as can be inferred by the messier city labels.

Early custom pizza boxes featured generic images printed with modular printing plates, which were filled in with a pizzeria's name and location to create a semi-custom design. Pizzerias could pick and choose from popular graphics like the boot of Italy, steaming pizza, a goofy chef, Italian flags, and simple borders. The ingredient border (*above and at right*) was introduced by Robert Aquilla of Converted Paper, a Brooklyn-based containerboard manufacturer, and Suzanne Stoner, a local artist, in the early 1970s. It became a popular graphic in the New York metropolitan area and, since it was never trademarked, several printers have either directly lifted or slightly modified the border for their own clients.

▶ This particular Ray's pizzeria was the first of many in Manhattan, predating all "famous" and "original" versions of the same name. It was located at 27 Prince Street from June 1959 to November 2011.

"RAY'S"

(EST.1959)

NEW YORK'S FINEST
GOURMET PIZZA

27 PRINCE STREET
NEW YORK, NY

966-1960

Always hot and delicious.

Fronte

made fresh just for you!

Rather than print their own, some pizzerias opt for generic boxes from their food distributors. It's not nearly as good for marketing their business but saves about 7 to 10 percent in printing costs. These generic boxes contain typical pizza imagery: Italian street scenes, pizza ingredients, checkered tablecloths, a slice or an entire pizza (always pepperoni), or any number of customer appreciation slogans.

▲ Restaurant supply distributor Cheney Brothers uses a coated outer liner for image crispness. The usual graphics are present, along with the addition of a brand name on the Chianti bottle (Fronte is a private label for pastas and pizzeria products sold by Cheney Brothers), a tactic popular with restaurant suppliers. This box is currently available in Cheney Brothers' distribution areas in the United States, the Caribbean, and Mexico.

▶ A similar stock box from the distributor Savona-Stavola uses not one, not two, but six phrases to extoll the product of their pizzeria clients and to thank customers for their patronage. This box is available in the distribution area around southern New Jersey, Pennsylvania, and Delaware.

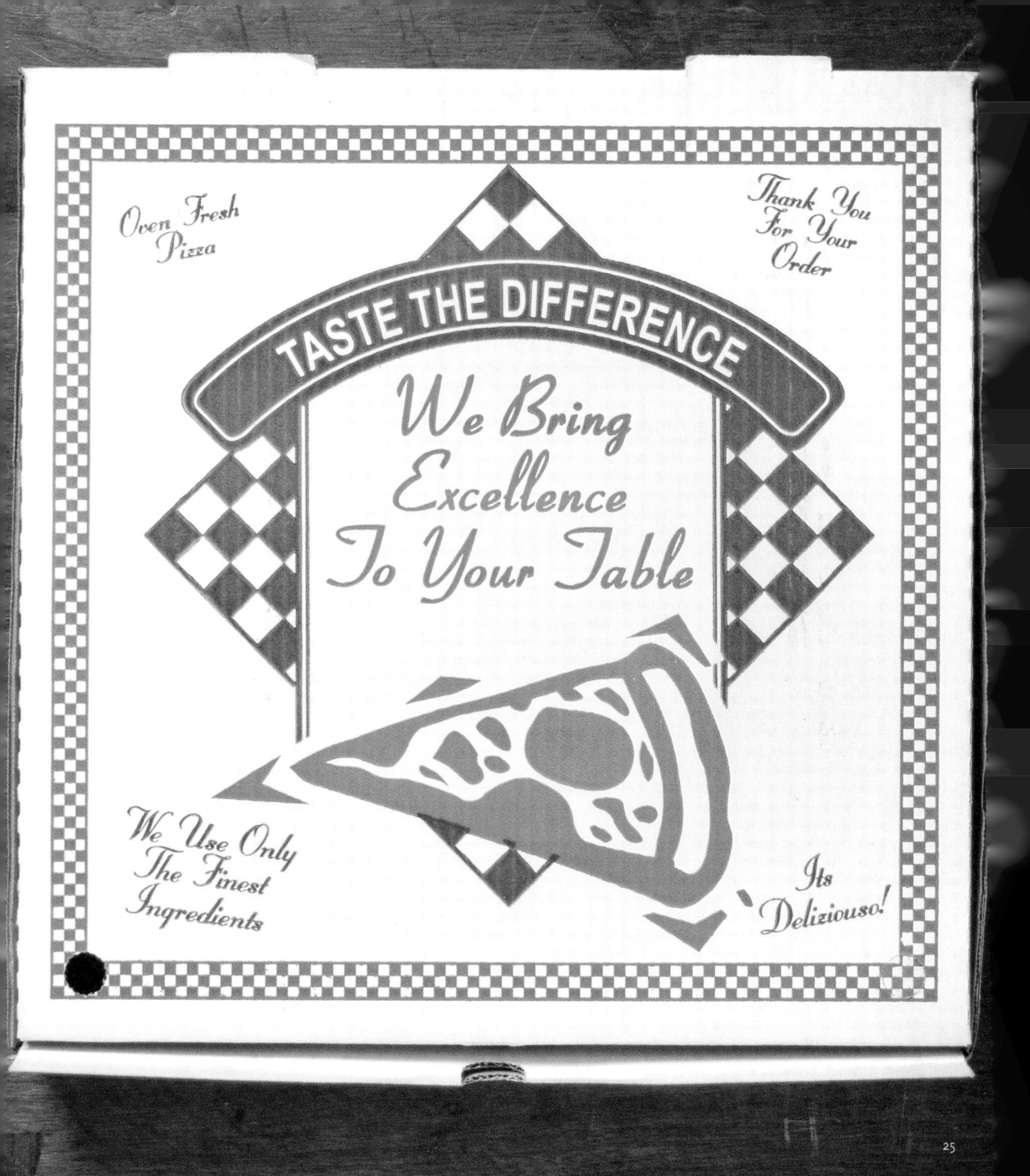
Oven Fresh Pizza
Thank You For Your Order
TASTE THE DIFFERENCE
We Bring Excellence To Your Table
We Use Only The Finest Ingredients
Its Deliziouso!

Oven Fresh Pizza

"Made from the finest ingredients"

BAG-AND-BOARD

Some old-school pizzerias still load their pizza onto a corrugated cardboard circle and then into a thin paper bag. The bag allows steam to escape, preventing soggy crust and the "cardboard" taste a box usually produces, but it offers no support for stacking pizzas unless paired with several Package Savers (see page 109). The New York pizza legend Patsy Grimaldi uses bags in his Brooklyn pizzeria, Juliana's, because they are less expensive, take up less space, and require no assembly as compared to standard boxes. East

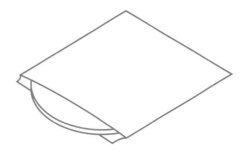

Boston's Santarpio's recently switched from bags to boxes because of customer demand for takeout pies, but staff and longtime customers prefer the old way.

◀ Pizza box manufacturer RockTenn estimates that 80 to 90 percent of all American pizza boxes are printed with two colors, the most popular of which are red and green. This stock box contains common elements of loose ingredients, a central pizza graphic, and the phrases "Oven Fresh" and "Made from the finest ingredients." The corrugated box's wide B fluting is amplified by vertical ink stripes, the "washboard effect," in which ink is collected along the ribs of a box's corrugated medium.

SAM'S
RESTAURANT & PIZZERIA
ITALIAN CUISINE

ORDERS
TO
TAKE OUT

238 COURT STREET • BROOKLYN, NY
Tel. 596-3458

WHO IS THE WINKING CHEF?

On July 2, 1997, a Croatian company called Podravka was denied a trademark for the popular image of a mustachioed, overweight, winking chef with his hand raised to his mouth in a gesture of approval. Even though the image had been commonplace for half a century, the Podravka application marked the first time a company attempted to claim ownership of this notorious piece of clip art.

The Nestlé corporation blocked Podravka's trademark attempt with evidence of a similar chef dating back to 1925, which it used on packages of sauce, pickles, and dehydrated snacks. Other companies used chef heads to lend credibility to their packaging, most notably Chef Boyardee as far back as 1928.

Crossover into the restaurant world didn't happen until after World War II, when chef caricatures become the image of choice for casual restaurants across the country. Menus for Rod's and Junior's, both Los Angeles burger joints, used cartoonish chefs in the 1950s. Junior's even adds the all-important wink. These chefs were overweight compared to their predecessors, a reflection of a postwar swing towards abundance. The Podravka image in particular has been in use at least as far back as 1956, when a hand-painted version was propped onto the roof of Schaller's Drive-In in Rochester, New York. The restaurant's founder claims to have copied it from a now-forgotten source.

Crossover into the pizza world likely happened when delivery service drove demand for printed mar-

This semi-custom box ◀ uses a nearly identical image to the one Podravka attempted to trademark in 1997. Notice the slight variations in sideburn length, mustache size, facial creases, and closure of the right eye between the face on this box and the one on page 30.

keting materials in the 1970s. Customers who called in orders from their homes needed menus and contact information for the pizzeria. To keep costs down, pizzerias opted for royalty-free stock images. Semi-custom clip-art-based boxes (see pages 22–23) were the most popular early images in the pizza business.

The chef on the roof of Schaller's has become the classic face of pizza boxes. But it doesn't stop there—examples of this same face appear across cultures with completely different cuisines.

But who is the man behind the face? Nobody really knows.

Sal's ITALIAN
Restaurant & Pizzeria

"You've Tried the Rest - Now Try the Best"

1440 S. Main Street
Blacksburg VA, 24060

(540) 953 - 4040

SalsBlacksburg.com

f Sals Blacksburg

It's only natural to think of your product as being better than that of the competition, but the phrase "you've tried all the rest, now try the best" is so overused it has become a parody of itself. Companies have attempted to trademark it for use in selling dried fruit, auto parts, chicken-wing sauce, limousine service, and fish bait, but its use on pizza boxes traces back to the 1960s with Lisanti Foods of Totowa, New Jersey.

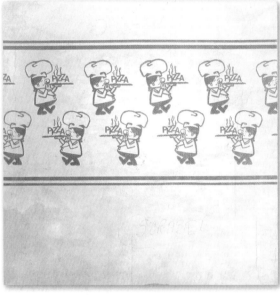

When a pizza box company's machines are idle between jobs, they run stock boxes to fill the gap. These generic boxes are similar to the distributor-owned variety but usually more anonymous, because the boxes are sold to multiple distributors and pizzerias and cannot call out brand names.

As if there were any question as to what these boxes contain, the inclusion of the word "pizza" serves to clarify. Red bricks suggest a brick oven, and loose ingredients connote freshness, but these boxes are produced without any knowledge of what type of oven or ingredients a pizzeria uses.

▲ Converted Paper experimented with continuous printing in the late 1970s. Rather than embed a single image across a pre-cut sheet, they printed an uninterrupted design onto a roll of paperboard. The process was abandoned as the industry shifted from paperboard to corrugated board.

FRESH
OVEN
BAKED ...

PIZZA

it's the Greatest!

CAN YOU RECYCLE A PIZZA BOX?

Unused pizza boxes are 100 percent recyclable, but you should think twice before you toss a used box into the recycling pile. Hundreds of millions of dollars are spent annually repairing recycling equipment from damage caused by contaminants in the waste stream—and pizza boxes are prime offenders. Leftover crusts and caked-on cheese can easily be removed, but greasy spots cannot. Check with your local recycling center to find out if they accept used pizza boxes. If they don't, simply cut out the offensive spots and recycle the rest.

Here's a quick guide to pizza-box recycling in major U.S. cities:

RECYCLE IT!
Boston
Chicago
Denver
Detroit
Miami
NYC
Pittsburgh

COMPOST IT!
Portland
San Francisco
Seattle

TRASH IT!
Anchorage
Atlanta
Austin
Baltimore
Charlotte
Dallas
Los Angeles
Nashville
New Orleans
Philadelphia
St. Louis
Salt Lake City

▶ This classic single-color image is sized to fit any box size in an effort to avoid the cost of multiple printing plates. The pizza chef in the lower left-hand corner is a stock image, but the pizzeria drawing was submitted by a loyal customer in the mid-1990s. This version of the box is no longer in print, as Ernie's has revised the claim of "specializing in pizza only" after expanding their menu in 2012.

ERNIE'S PIZZERIA

Same Folks Serving You and Yours Since 1971

1279 WHALLEY AVENUE   WESTVILLE

SPECIALIZING IN PIZZA ONLY
Beer & Wine Served On Premise

BEFORE YOU LEAVE YOUR HOME

CALL IN YOUR ORDER

PHONE 387-3362

SCENES

THE CAFÉ SCENE

Storefront scenes are popular on generic stock boxes. They illustrate the quaint atmosphere associated with mom-and-pop establishments. Common elements include a labeled awning, a "specials" board, and window plants. The most common element, a vacant table set for two, is almost welcoming.

These examples illustrate three different printing methods. At right, we see a two-color spot print on a white top liner. The white background creates a crisp image that pops off the box without the need for additional color or shading. Kraft liners provide the backgrounds for both images above, necessitating additional color and shading. RockTenn's approach ▲ uses a dot screen to achieve variations in the application of black ink to the substrate. The most complex print is the version from Roma Foods (*above left*), which reveals greater depth and detail thanks to the more refined process printing and the addition of white ink. (See also page 94.)

© 2011 Star Pizza Box of Florida, Inc.

PIZZERIA

PIZZERIA

TODAY'S SPECIAL

OPEN

39

This array of street scenes displays various degrees of activity. Notice the contrast between the bustling neighborhood in this full color Italian scene and the desolate courtyard with a dry fountain in the two-color American design.

PIZZAPOCALYPSE

When the Italian food distributor Ferraro Foods needed a new design for their stock boxes in 2007, they looked no further than their own receptionist Tamikee Jennings. Having recently completed a degree in visual communications at Gibbs College in Livingston, New Jersey, Jennings jumped at the opportunity to expand her portfolio beyond the usual business cards, logos, and CD covers. Her only instruction was to produce something original and warm focused on pizza. The result, Jennings's first pizza box design, has been one of the most popular pizza boxes in the Northeast since its introduction in 2007.

The scene is quite ominous, but early sketches included children playing in the street and a pizza delivery boy in the foreground. These elements were removed to keep the focus on the pizzeria. According to the artist, the looming pizza is either rising or setting depending on the viewer's interpretation, suggesting that pizza has no time constraints.

One of the more unusual components of the image is the inclusion of Jennings's signature in the lower right-hand corner. "The CEO felt that it was unlike any other pizza box image he had seen," she says, "so he was very adamant about wanting me to be recognized for my work."

Because of its ubiquity in the New York area, "Pizza Town" has appeared in more than a dozen films and television shows. Jennings was particularly excited to see her work in an episode of MTV's *Run's House*, as well as in the movie *The Sorcerer's Apprentice*, starring Nicolas Cage. It is by far her most successful piece of art in terms of production and reach.

The Pizza Town box is printed for Ferraro by Pratt Industries, which specializes in 100 percent recycled pizza boxes. Their New York City facility mills its own paper from locally sourced curbside recycling (called Old Corrugated Containers, or OCC) and produces corrugated board in-house. Huge barges transport bundles of used paper products to Pratt's mill via the Arthur Kill, a tidal strait that separates Staten Island and New Jersey. Their production is so large they often sell excess paper inventory to competitors.

Similar stock designs from Whalen Packaging ▲ and
RockTenn ◀ feature framed street scenes. Unlike most
other stock boxes, these two feature people in their
scenes.

In the summer of 2011, Larry Santora, the owner of Picasso's Pizzeria in Buffalo, New York, commissioned the local artist Michael Biondo to create this image of an inviting Italian village. The original piece was created with pastels and photographed for reproduction as a four-color process print. The chalkboard sign reads, "HE WHO FINDS PICASSO'S FINDS A TREASURE."

The image went through dozens of drafts before it was ready for production. The grapevine in the upper right-hand corner underwent massive changes, even becoming a tomato vine at one point in the process. Biondo originally intended to keep the art gallery doors open (building on left) with a full display of paintings inside, but in the end decided against it so as not to distract the viewer from Picasso's Pizzeria.

The box features none of the usual marketing elements like a phone number or street address; even the name of the pizzeria is tucked covertly into the image. Santora realized that his customers would have no need of his phone number once a box was in their hands, so he decided to produce images that would be special unto themselves, as pieces of art, rather than resorting to direct marketing. It's a real collectible, and Picasso's fans save the box rather than condemn it to the recycling pile. It also has the artist's signature in the lower right-hand corner. Available at a cost of $0.99 per box, it's a very affordable piece of art.

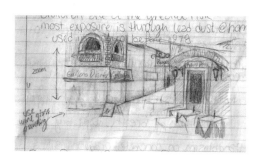

◀ Biondo sketched his first draft while attending a construction safety course.

HOT & DELICIOUS

PIZZA

MADE JUST FOR YOU...

STAR PIZZA BOXES

Most corrugated-box companies dedicate only a portion of their efforts to producing pizza boxes, but the aptly named Star Pizza Boxes focuses on a single product. Hal Porter, who formerly worked at a restaurant distribution company and even had his own pizzeria in Ohio, founded the company in 1990. Thanks to Porter's deep understanding of the industry, Star is able to provide a much-needed service to independent pizzerias. In an industry that cuts pennies by outsourcing, Star proudly makes all their boxes in the USA.

▲ From Sorrento Pizzeria in Lakeland, Florida, where Star Pizza is headquartered.

◄ The behind-the-scenes concept first appears in 1998 with a stock box design from Star Pizza Boxes called "Red Brick." Founder and president Hal Porter worked with a local artist/part-time grocery store clerk to create the image, which is estimated to have been printed more than 1 billion times to date. It gives a cartoonish glimpse behind the scenes at your local pizzeria, with a reminder that the box's contents were "made just for you . . ."

▲ A similar design appeared a decade later (2008) on this cult favorite generic box. Although its creator isn't marked on the box, the bottle of olive oil on the table and cans on the background shelves hint at its origin. Supremo Italiano, Isabella, and Qualite are all house brands owned by the restaurant supply wholesaler Jetro/Restaurant Depot. This box appears only west of the Rocky Mountains and contains one of the greatest phrases to have ever appeared on a pizza box, referring not to the food within but to life itself.

▲ Custom business card for Converted Paper's founder, printed with the same red ink that was used on early printed pizza boxes.

◀ Greek-owned pizzerias often prefer blue as the accent color on stock boxes.

FREEPORT PAPER

After World War II, Pasquale Trilli returned to his father-in-law's printing company in Brooklyn to put to use the mechanical knowledge he'd picked up in the U.S. Navy. Eagle National Printing produced cards for earrings and costume jewelry but had trouble producing the volume that would make the company competitive in the industry. Trilli tweaked the machinery to run twelve cards at a time, four times the prior capacity, and the business grew. By the mid-1950s, Eagle National Printing became Converted Paper, with a move from lower Manhattan to the Brooklyn waterfront, and expanded into the bakery box business. Profiting from the bakery market was difficult, because they were getting small orders for too many different-size boxes, so Converted Paper directed its efforts toward products with fewer options. Trilli approached a nearby pizzeria on Columbia Street and Hamilton Avenue in 1955 with an offer to print custom boxes for just 5 cents apiece. A large pizza was just 25 cents at the time, and because

the owner didn't want any additional expenses, he declined. Luckily for Converted Paper, a competitor of the first pizzeria saw the marketing benefit of a printed box and placed an order with Trilli's company. The concept caught on, and printed pizza boxes became standard in pizzerias throughout New York City and the northeastern United States.

Business grew and partnerships changed, but Converted Paper continues to operate as Freeport Paper, based in Long Island, New York.

◀ Freeport Paper's current stock box was designed in 2008 by the company's senior production designer Holly Del Re, based on a painting by the artist Betty Whiteaker. Although it has no official title, the image is affectionately known within the company as "Saks Fifth Avenue" or, more simply, "Café." The pizza maker in the bottom left-hand corner has been a trademark of Freeport Paper since the 1970s.

While most American boxes are converted with the spot-printing method, European containers often use process printing to achieve a full-color spectrum.

These two boxes feature nearly identical pizzas with whole black olives, a rare sight on American pizzas.

ROCKTENN

RockTenn is by far the largest pizza box manufacturer in the United States. They operate seventeen corrugated plants, two of which are dedicated pizza box facilities. The location in Wakefield, Massachusetts, is capable of producing 1 million pizza boxes in a single day. Roughly half their business comes from the Big Four (Pizza Hut, Domino's, Papa John's, and Little Caesar's), but the remainder goes through distributors to regional chains and mom-and-pop stores. RockTenn currently produces 8 billion square feet of corrugated paperboard per year, the equivalent of 380 American football fields per day, which accounts for 65 percent of all pizza boxes in the United States.

▶ In the late 1990s, Roma Foods introduced a series of pizza boxes that featured typical scenes from different Italian cities. The first-edition image of Venice was RockTenn's first four-color pizza box, which opened the floodgates for box-top image design. The year it debuted at the International Pizza Expo in Las Vegas, Roma Foods purchased 600,000 pieces. The substrate itself is an E flute material, which experiences less compression and therefore produces a cleaner print than its B flute counterpart.

Ponte Vecchio - Florence, Italy

▲ This "Tour of Italy: Third Edition" box labels Florence on the lid because the Ponte Vecchio isn't as recognizable as other Italian landmarks.

Page 56, "Harvest." Stock boxes devoid of any reference to Italy or pizza are extremely rare.

Page 57, "Season's Greetings." This box earned a bronze medal at the International Flexographic Printing Competition for RockTenn's Wakefield facility in 1998.

Page 58, "Pizza by the Bay." The image of pizza on a table accompanied by a glass of wine appears on countless boxes. It serves as an invitation to the consumer, almost a preview of what comforts await beyond the corrugated boundary. Regardless of any variations between images, artists seem to agree that red wine is the perfect beverage pairing for pizza.

Page 59, "Rolling Hills" by RockTenn for Sysco. This scene of a California vineyard sold more than 1 million pieces in 1998 alone.

Season's Greetings

SEASONAL BOXES

▲ In the mid-1990s, Roma Foods celebrated the introduction of four-color printing with a series of seasonal boxes. The designs are lighthearted and fun, each presenting a visual joke. One of the earliest in the series was a Christmas box depicting Santa dropping pizzas off the back of a packed sled. Originally, the bumper sticker read "WE BRAKE FOR PIZZA," but it was replaced with an American flag following the events of September 11, 2001.

◀ Continuing with the seasonal schedule, Roma introduced a Superbowl-themed box the following year. More than 3 million pizzas are delivered on Superbowl Sunday, making it the pizza industry's busiest day. Since Roma is based in New Jersey, they chose team colors that could potentially represent all local teams. Green covers both the Jets and the Eagles, while blue suggests the Giants and Patriots.

▶ This Valentine's Day box (circa 1996) is one of the only Roma boxes that does not feature a company logo.

American boxes often focus on Italy, with images of the Tower of Pisa, the Coliseum, and Venetian gondolas, but Italian boxes concentrate specifically on Naples, pizza's birthplace. These two Neapolitan street scenes depict pizza being eaten by hand, as was necessary for consumers who were often too poor to afford utensils.

The box at the left features pizza sold in the streets by a vendor, probably the son of a local baker who only baked the breads as a means of getting rid of old dough. Judging by the use of mozzarella and tomato in both images, the scenes likely take place in the early to mid-nineteenth century. According to the 1835 travel diary of Alexandre Dumas: "The pizza is prepared with bacon, with lard, with cheese, with tomatoes, with fish. It is the gastronomic thermometer of the market. The price of pizza rises and falls according to the rate of the ingredients just designated."

TYPOGRAPHY
& DESIGN

New York's Farinella Bakery had to contract specialty corrugated box company Jersey Paper Plus to produce a container for their nearly four-foot pizza. The style comes from Rome, where it is referred to as *pizza al metro* and often sold by the slice, priced according to its weight.

The beauty of repetition enhances these simple text-
based designs from Pizzanista (Los Angeles) and an
Italian stock box.

ED HARDY

Artist Ed Hardy was a fan of Tony's Pizza Napoletana in the North Beach section of San Francisco long before he designed this limited-edition box. The four-color spot print by Star Pizza Boxes was limited to a run of 10,000 and sold to customers for $3 on top of their pizza purchase. Proceeds were split evenly between three local charities: the Harqua Foundation, Basketball City, and St. Anthony's Kitchen. This particular box is one of the 350 signed by Hardy himself.

Ed Hardy is best known for the multi-platform brand that sports his name, but his work stems from an incredibly influential career in body art. The design here is a modified tattoo: crossed pizza peels in place of the more traditional crossed anchors; the tiger and dragon personify Japanese power symbols; the giant eagle represents classic Americana and a pizza sits in the center of it all.

When pizzeria owner Tony Gemignani approached him with the idea to do a pizza box, Hardy was excited about using the unusual creative medium. After clearing the project with his eponymous brand's legal team, Hardy's only challenge was to create a design that would work within the four-color limit. He called the project "the cherry on the sundae of a great career!"

▲ To celebrate his pizzeria's fiftieth anniversary, Aldo Evangelista ordered a limited run of 5,000 commemorative boxes. The golden liner increased La Hacienda's price-per-box over 30 percent above an already steep 70 cents. But, as Aldo says, "A nice pizza needs a nice box."

Unlike the standard heavy-duty American pizza box, this one is an ultra-thin E flute with a virgin-white inner liner and a coated outer liner. The inner liner doesn't break down under humidity, and the outer liner provides a smooth surface for sharp printing. The image on the box predates the restaurant, which used the graphic before it was converted from a bar/fish fry into a pizzeria in 1957.

▶ Rather than use tired clip art with boring text, Tony Boloney's in Atlantic City, New Jersey, opts for a completely customized image. Designed by the owner Mike Hauke, the image presents a new take on the infamous mustachioed chef and avoids the obvious red-and-green color pairing in favor of a bright blue. Hauke's cartoon artist friend drew the logo and lettering specifically for use on this box.

Atlantic City's Original.

Tony Boloney's ™

ATLANTIC CITY'S BEST PIZZA & MOST CREATIVE GRUB

TONYBOLONEYS.COM - 609-344-TONY - 300 ORIENTAL AVE/VERMONT AVE -ATLANTIC CITY, NJ

Famous Stuffed Pizza

Restaurant and Pizzeria

CHOSEN BEST
CHICAGO TRIBUNE
NEW YORK TIMES
CHICAGO MAGAZINE
NBC TV

Trademarked names are the focus of these two
custom boxes.

ENJOY DELIGHTFUL MEALS **DINE OUT**

Snack Headquarters-

PIZZATOWN, U.S.A., Is An Excellent New Drive-In Spot On Rt. 46, East Paterson–Serves Delicious Food

New Enterprise Offers Tasty, Delectable Italian Specialties Home Made Style, Made To Order, At Most Reasonable Prices

The gay, brightly colored, attractive Pizza-town, U.S.A., now open on Rte. 46, just across the Passaic River in East Paterson, near the Garden State Parkway, has found a ready acceptance among the lovers of good Italian food specialties of the area, and is doing a thriving business.

Gayly bedecked in red, white, and blue, with a brightly painted "Uncle Sam" as its identifying insignia, its premises are spotless inside and out. Outdoor table facilities are protected by a pastel colored canopy extended beyond the actual building, which provides shade or cover from sun and rain.

The popular priced menu is limited, the management preferring to specialize in a few, well prepared "always-fresh" items rather than to try to offer a wide selection of dishes which might produce waste and force up the prices.

Since "pizza" has become so popular in the past few years, it is only natural that this excellent roadside spot should offer that famous snack which has replaced the frankfurter as America's most popular dish. Unfortunately "pizza" is sold on practically every corner in the country-most of it poor, much of it indifferent in quality. The number of places which serve a really good pizza is very small, and folks hereabouts will be happy to go to a little distance to get the best, we are certain! Good pizza is truly a tasty thing-crisp and savory, while inferior pizza isn't really worth eating. Pizzatown, U.S.A. is one of the few places we have found which serves first quality pizza-from fresh home-made dough, and premium flour, yeast, spices, oil, cheese, tomatoes, and

Tempting Treats - of all kinds, served at the new Pizzatown, U.S.A., located just across the Passaic River, on Route 46, in East Paterson

ingredients such as anchovies, sausage, etc. Pizza is available fresh, crisp and bubbly, savory at Pizzatown, U.S.A., by the slice (at 15¢) or in 2 sizes at $1.00, and $1.50.

Sandwich items-all excellent include hot sausage, peppers, meatball, peppers and eggs. A large selection of authentic Italian ices, and delicious soft drinks are also offered.

Special mention must be made of two traditional Italian specialties of the house rarely seen in this area anymore. A special pie called Calzone, which resembles an apple turnover in appearance is prepared in snack size for 35¢, and family size for $1.50. Calzone, for the uninitiated, is concocted mainly of fresh pot cheese, Virginia ham, parmesan and mozzarella cheese, olive oil and subtle special

seasoning, which is placed on one half of a freshly prepared pizza shell. The shell is then "turned over" and crimped to seal in the delicious filling. A small hole is poked into the top of the shell-a swirlslice of mozzarella inserted for a flourish, and the top lightly olive oiled. It is then ready for the oven. When taken out after eight minutes, the result at Pizzatown, U.S.A. is a beautifully browned large hot pie, fragrant and delicious a perfect take home meal for the entire family or to be eaten on the spot. Nourishing, tasty and tender, it is also available with generous slices of pure pork sausage added (50¢ extra).

If you like crullers, you are certain to enjoy Zeppoli, home-made here, another tradit

ional Italian style item, which resembles a conventional cruller, but is less sweet and has its own characteristic appetizing flavor, 5¢ each, or to take home a bag full 6 for 25¢.

Cold sandwiches with tomato and lettuce of Italian salami, Capacola, proscutto, Bologna, provolone and American cheese, or in combination are also excellent here. Stop by with the family for a snack, or take home a bag or box of delicious goodies, either will make you popular with your family as a person who knows fine food, and where to obtain it. The patronage is basically solid family trade, although it is very popular with the youngsters at the nearby Gantner Ave. Public School (some 250 of whom attended a special "End of Semester Party" there on school closing day). The kids enjoy themselves at Pizzatown, U.S.A., but behave themselves, and do not bother the other patrons-the management here has a way with the youngsters.

Many nearby lodges and clubs send a committee over for hot collations which are brought back for the members after meetings repast or quick pickup orders, call Swarthmore 7-6172.

Pizzatown, U.S.A. is open to serve you from 10 am to midnight seven days a week. Try this new spot soon.

Ray Tomo is an enterprising gentleman who has brought us this good drive in restaurant.

The recipes have been used in the family for three generations.

Try his wares-you'll learn to call him "Friend!"

FOR QUICK PICK-UP

ELMWOOD PARK, N.J.
(201) 797-6172

Rather than print an unattributed claim the way most pizzerias do, Pizzatown U.S.A. in Elmwood Park, New Jersey, gives us a 1958 review announcing their opening. The pizzeria's owners printed the review with blue ink on a bleached outer liner to match Pizzatown's patriotic color scheme. The original newspaper page used a different Italian chef in its header; these winking chefs were added for use on the box.

World Famous

"Welcome to Regina Pizza!" Since 1926, over eighty five years, these words have greeted customers in the North End of Boston. When the Polcari Family took over Pizzeria Regina on Thatcher Street, they made it what it is today, the Oldest Pizza House in New England. For four generations, Regina's delicious pizza has been inspired by love of good food and the special pride of the Polcari family. The Original Regina Pizza had a Neapolitan crust topped with a hearty blend of fine cheese, flavorful sauce, delicate seasoning, and the finest toppings. Back then, Anthony Polcari did it all ...made pizza, tended bar, waited on tables, and washed the dishes. Anthony made a lot of friends and his insistence on quality kept them coming back for more. Anthony believed there were no short cuts to excellence. His claim of years ago, "I give the best that I can make" is as true today as it was in generations past. His secret was simple: every day we will start with the freshest and the finest ...the freshest vegetables and meats, the finest recipes and care ...no preservatives, no additives ...just fresh, natural foods cooked to perfection and combined with treasured family pride and tradition. Since those early days, the faces have changed. But the Polcari family still keeps a watchful eye over it all. It is as important to the family today that Regina pizza is the best that can be made, the best you can buy. The family wants you to be happily satisfied. It's a matter of great pride and family tradition here at the Oldest Pizza House in New England.

Since 1926 Regina Pizzeria
BOSTON'S BRICKOVEN PIZZA

The "Oldest Pizza House in New England" has a lot to say about its history and attention to quality. The QR code in the upper right-hand corner is a recent trend in pizza box design.

These boxes make great use of overprinting to achieve
darker colors from combining two lighter inks.

PORTRAITS

The proud chef is a common motif in pizza box top imagery. Its use spans the globe but finds its most abundant appearances on generic stock boxes across Europe and the United States. Two main patterns exist within this genre: the post-bake presentation and the mid-bake pose (see pages 84–85, 122, and 131).

Common elements in the post-bake presentation include the background of a wood-fired brick oven, ingredients around the perimeter, an overweight chef, the finished product, and the word "pizza." Both examples above exhibit the pattern in full color but their American counterpart ▶ is a much simpler two-color version. Notice the difference in features between the European and American examples.

The image serves the same purpose as the ever popular "You've tried the rest, now try the best" phrase (see pages 30–31). It's all about pride in one's product, even if the box was created by someone who has never tasted it.

PIZZA

OVEN FRESH

The visual gag of displaying a smaller version of a picture within itself is called the Droste Effect. Named for the Dutch brand of cocoa powder that began using the effect in ads as far back as 1904, the Droste Effect has in fact been employed to various degrees since medieval times.

Listed as "Bandanna" on the website of the Italian pizza box producer Liner Italia, this image features a pizza maker who bears a striking resemblance to the American actor George Clooney. Sightings of the box have been reported in Germany, Bosnia, Ireland, Hungary, and the Canary Islands.

The print is a four-color process made on an HD Flexo machine.

CIANCIO

Luca Ciancio fell into the pizza box business in 1998 when a friend asked him for a pizza box illustration that went beyond standard fare. The result was a three-color Valentine's Day box, which brought more requests for Ciancio's unique work. He has since produced illustrations for more than 250 pizza boxes.

In order to manage image composition, Ciancio starts each project as an eight-by-eight- or ten-by-ten-centimeter (approximately four-inch) sketch. He then creates the final image using either acrylic or watercolor because they dry quickly, producing instant results. Some pieces call for additional modification by airbrushing, but Ciancio tries to avoid digital tweaking. "I prefer to use traditional techniques," he says, "because pizza is traditional." The final piece is vibrant, clear, and often suggests a deeper story.

Thanks to Ciancio's contributions to pizza box art, the entire medium has evolved. It's a stark contrast to the more economical two-color prints common in the United States. Ciancio reasons that the difference is cultural: "Here we breathe art and creativity in every corner. What we lack is the ability to transform into 'business,' which is much better for you Americans."

▶ Here, a clever Ciancio design incorporates the necessary "pizza" tag inside the universe of the image's characters rather than having it stamped at the top. For more of Ciancio's work, see pages 62–63 and 87–91.

The city of Naples is often represented by Pulcinella, the jester-like figure dressed in white with a long-nosed black mask. The Neapolitan mascot is usually portrayed as an incorrigible joker, yet these two depictions appear to be alternate renditions. ◄ Here, we see a tender moment with Pulcinella wooing a young woman with a song.

▲ Above, Luca Ciancio presents the usually male character as female, titling the piece "Pulcinellina." This provocative Italian box is a popular attraction at pizza trade shows and insures return customers for takeout and delivery at Via Tribunali, a Neapolitan-style pizzeria with locations in Seattle and New York City.

ANTONIO DE CURTIS

Each of these three boxes features the Neapolitan actor Antonio De Curtis. Better known by his stage name Totò, De Curtis made a name for himself with comedic performances in mid-twentieth-century films. His work earned him comparisons to Buster Keaton and Charlie Chaplin, but De Curtis's talents spread across the spectrum from writing to singing to poetry and everything in between.

▲ First we see Totò sharing a pizza and a beer with Massimo Troisi, an actor who drew inspiration from Totò but never worked with him. ▲ Next we have Peppino De Filippo, who famously played opposite Totò on numerous occasions throughout the 1950s. Finally, ▶ Totò appears with the most famous Neapolitan actress, Sophia Loren, whose career began in the 1950s and continues today. In all three boxes, Totò seems to be fixated on his costar and is never himself holding the pizza.

Tony's New York Pizza

www.tonyspizzahouston.com

Here are two takes on the image of a pizza maker tossing dough, one from the United States and the other found in Belgium (but printed in Italy).

The act of tossing dough originated in the United States, where higher protein levels in wheat flour produced more elastic dough than its European predecessor. Pizza makers flaunted their dough's strength by throwing it in the air. Pizza dough acrobatics is now an international sport exhibited at pizza trade shows and events around the world.

▲ Full-color images like this usually use four-color-process printing with cyan, magenta, yellow, and black. The low-resolution look of this particular box is a result of eliminating the black component in an effort to lower printing costs.

HOW ARE PIZZA BOXES PRINTED?

SPOT PRINTING transfers images to paperboard with continuous blocks of ink. The result is a simple print with any detail being produced by halftone screens. Each color in a design is split into its own printing plate. Colors can be overprinted or knocked out depending on the intended result. Most pizza boxes are printed with this method because it's the least expensive. (See pages 30–31.)

More detailed compositions with a full color spectrum are produced by **PROCESS PRINTING**. This method separates an image into four components: cyan, magenta, yellow, and black (CMYK). Each color is applied to the substrate as variously sized dots to form complete images when printed together. A close look at the image reveals a pattern in which each of the four inks has its own place. (See page 47.)

The sharpest photo-quality prints are achieved through **PRE-PRINT**, the conversion of outer liner before corrugation occurs. Since ink is applied to a flat page, it avoids the problem presented by cushioned corrugated board. This is the highest quality but also the highest cost for pizza box printing. (See page 108.)

▶ This piece, created in Italy but discovered in Amsterdam, sports images that seem to resemble popular television characters from *The Simpsons*, although some very significant details appear to have been changed to avoid legal complications. The Bart character has facial hair and covers his trademark spikes with a cap. Homer's counterpart sports a tattoo and a full head of hair. Note the soccer jersey hanging on the wall; the number ten is significant in the sport's history for having been worn by many of its greatest players, including Pelé and Diego Maradona.

INTERACTIVE
& HIGH-TECH

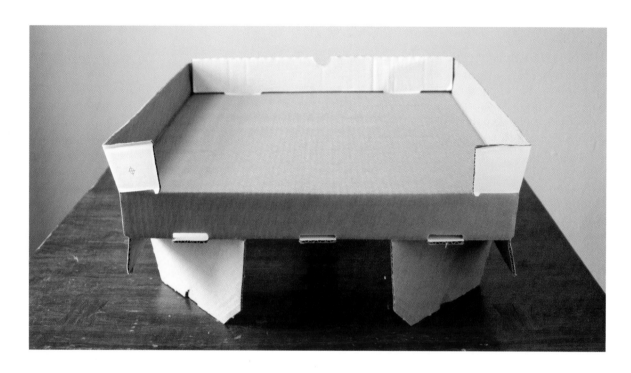

In 2009, Andrew DePascale and Marcello Mandreucci invented a space-saving solution for cluttered pizza-eating situations. This box transforms into a serving stand to free up table space that would normally be eaten up by the box's footprint. Perforated regions of the lid fold out to connect with tabs on the side and front flaps, lifting the box base six inches off the surface. Since the box is not losing heat by direct conduction, the pizza theoretically stays hotter longer than it would if sitting directly on a table.

FROM YOUR FAVORITE PIZZERIA

THANK YOU
PLEASE CALL AGAIN

TABLE BOX INSTRUCTIONS

STEP 1
OPEN BOX
&
POKE HOLES

STEP 2
PULL IN LEGS
&
LOCK IN WALLS

STEP 3
FOLD LID UNDER
&
SERVE!

GREENBOX™
Our Planet • Our Responsibility

FREE!!
Plates & Storage Container
SEE INSTRUCTIONS

This just may be the most talked-about innovation in pizza box history. A custom die pattern creates perforations that allow the lid to split into four serving plates, and the base becomes a storage container for leftover slices. Beyond this automatic secondary use, the perforations make it easy to break the box down for disposal once it has exhausted its usefulness. Pizzerias can give customers the benefits of a GreenBox for no additional cost over that of conventional corrugated boxes.

The GreenBox's stock graphic creates a visual pun with the pizza slice/evergreen tree to stress the "green" theme, but the artwork is completely customizable.

JOHN CORRELL

Over the course of eighteen years, John Correll developed more than forty unique pizza box structures, and holds more pizza box patents than anyone else. He has a long track record of working in the pizza industry, starting with a position at the sixth Domino's store in Lansing, Michigan, way back in 1967. Correll became a consultant for the growing chain and launched his own pizzeria in 1976 called Pizzuti's Pizza. His concept was to offer only eight-inch personal pizzas and Coca-Cola.

Correll first entered the box business in the late 1980s when he received a blank in the mail from a consulting client who wanted help marketing a new pizza box he invented. It was designed to break down into a storage container for leftover slices. (The box on the opposite page is a variation on this concept.) Although the design was brilliant, big pizza chains were averse to spending the extra penny per box to cover production. Correll realized that the only way to convince the big chains to take on a new product would be to make it cheaper. Since 70 percent of a box's production cost goes to raw material, Correll started working to engineer a box that required less paper to produce.

Correll's first patent application was filed in 1993 for a tab-lock box. Within the next ten years he was granted thirty-three patents for food cartons, the most lucrative of which was a design called Matable Bank and Food Carton (patent #5,752,651). Domino's began using the box design in 1998 for packaging breadsticks and Stuffed Cheesy Bread. Correll left the world of pizza box engineering shortly after Domino's replaced his Matable design in 2008.

◀ ▲ New Zealand–based Hell Pizza's box has a central perforated section that separates to become a perfectly branded coffin-shaped container "for your remains."

This elegant two-color design doubles as an interactive game when the left lid flap is upturned. Players fling bits of crust over the box's left field wall. Affectionately known as the Green Monster, Fenway Park's actual left field wall is 37 feet and 2 inches tall and boasts in its proximity the most coveted seats in baseball. The field's odd contours are the result of Fenway's cramped position within Boston's tight urban landscape.

This box was available from Boston-based Papa Gino's during the 2012 baseball season.

PIZZA

Italian Landmark Collection

VENICE · ITALY

HOT DELICIOUS & FUN

The Venetian scene on this box lid is actually an eighty-piece puzzle. The concept comes courtesy of a now-defunct company called PackToy, who planned to sell the boxes as an added value for pizzeria customers.

Other options included boxes that could transform into a soccer field, a dinosaur statue, or a model airplane. Sadly, production costs kept the boxes out of reach for most operators.

In late 2009, Domino's Pizza shipped 23 million pizza boxes featuring three different Hasbro games: Cranium, Pictureka, and Connect 4 × 4. The boxes were part of a cross-promotional effort to market the game company's Family Game Night promotion. An extensive TV and online campaign encouraged families to play board games together, and Domino's presented itself as the perfect dinner complement.

The lid's side panels house removable pieces that can be used for gameplay directly on the box top. This variation of the popular game allows for four players (it was originally intended for only two) by using four sets of dual-colored tokens. When a player places a token on the board, it can also be used by her opponent, whose color is likewise displayed. Each piece can therefore be used by two different players in their competing races toward victory.

The shape of the box points to a design patented by Weyerhaeuser Company in 1997 that uses angled front corners. This increases stacking strength while simultaneously securing the pizza, and decreases paper use.

Domino's® feat. 初音ミク
HATSUNE MIKU

piapro Illustration by ＳＳＩ /Crypton Future Media, Inc. www.piapro.net

ネット注文なら5%OFF!! http://www.dominos.jp/ ドミノピザ 検索

PACKAGE SAVER

Children tend to think of it as a little white dollhouse table, but the white plastic tripod inside your pizza box has an important function. The Package Saver was patented by first-time inventor and Long Island resident Carmela Vitale in 1985. From patent 4,498,586:

> A temperature-resistant molded plastic device is described for use in boxes or packages such as pizza boxes where there is a tendency of large cover portions to sag downwardly to damage the soft pizza or other packaged products.

Millions of Package Savers are sold every year for the cost of about 1 cent per piece, but the rising popularity of corrugated Walker-style and corner-cut boxes are leading to its decline.

◄ Domino's Japan launched a stunning campaign in March 2013 featuring this bizarre box. The character in the center, Hatsune Miku, is a singing synthesizer application with a humanoid persona. She can be programmed to make human vocalizations with a built-in sound bank. Hatsune Miku has appeared in commercials, a television series, and even projected on stage for live performances.

The magic of this box becomes apparent when it is paired with an exclusive Domino's Japan iPhone app. The free app uses the iPhone's video interface to generate an image of Hatsune Miku performing atop the pizza box. By changing the angle of capture, users can manipulate their view of the performance.

The box was so popular that the first run sold out in just six days. As of this writing, the Hatsune Miku app is available only on iPhone and only in Japanese. And it seems to work only with this one pizza box.

ROSSOPOMODORO®

PRESENTS

LA PIZZA NAPOLETANA T.S.G.*
*(Traditional Specialty Guaranteed) denomination

THE "CORNICIONE"
(LITERALLY THE BIG FRAME)
MUST BE AT LEAST
0.4-0.8 INCH HIGH.

FRESH TOMATO
OR SAN MARZANO
PEELED TOMATOES

PDO (PRODUCT
DENOMINATION OF ORIGIN)
BUFFALO MOZZARELLA
OR MOZZARELLA T.S.G.*

SOFT
AND ELASTIC HEART

BAKED IN THE TRADITIONAL
340 BRICKS WOOD BURNING
OVEN

NEAPOLITAN
EXTRA-VIRGIN
OLIVE OIL

THE DIAMETER SHOULD NOT BE OVER 14 INCH

produced for

EATALY
alti cibi

LA MOZZARELLA
DI BUFALA CAMPANA
E IL FIORDILATTE

I POMODORI
SAN MARZANO

IL CUORE
NAPOLETANO

L'OLIO
EXTRAVERGINE D'OLIVA

LA FARINA
DI NAPOLI

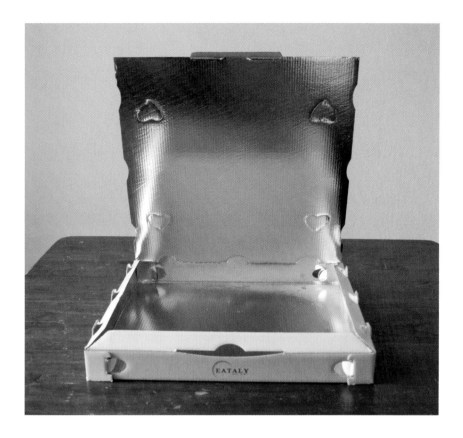

This Euro lock box features seventeen discrete vents for steam release, four of which double as structural stabilizers. Exciting as that may be, the container's interior holds its true innovation by way of a metallic polyester lining that both conducts heat and prevents the paper component from absorbing oil. Water-soluble glue bonds the metallic coating to the inner liner, making separation simple for recyclability.

Because of its advanced features, this technology runs double the price of a standard corrugated pizza box. Nonetheless, its inventors at INPACT (Italy) believe it will succeed with high-end restaurants who understand the necessity for quality products to travel in quality containers.

The photo-quality graphic is preprinted on the box's outer liner with a description of Pizza Napoletana T.S.G., the European Union's designation for authentic Neapolitan pizza. Requirements of Pizza Napoletana T.S.G. include specific Italian ingredients, intense baking methods, and predetermined crust height.

The VENTiT Box by Shree Krishna Packaging (India) tackles the Holy Grail of pizza box ventilation: allowing crust-damaging steam to escape without sacrificing necessary heat. The box does so by exposing sections of the corrugated medium in alternating segments inside and outside the box, allowing moisture to escape through the fluted channels of the medium. Manufacturing the box involves a slight rearrangement of traditional corrugated box construction but requires no new technology. A standard box's three layers are usually combined, printed, and then cut. The VENTiT method calls for the joining of the medium and inner liner, then cuts the two together before combining it with a precut, preprinted outer liner.

Shree Krishna's owner, Vinay Mehta, said he "was blessed with the idea" after thirty-five years in the corrugated industry. The invention has since won several design awards, including first place in the "Form and Function" category at the 2011 Association of Independent Corrugated Converters Awards in Las Vegas. The AICC has not honored any other pizza box before or since.

Currently available only in Mumbai and Dubai, VENTiT has the potential to drastically improve the quality of delivery pizza.

Pizza Hut

At the time you receive this pizza, if the hot spot does not say HOT, your next pizza is FREE*

Hot Spot*

Did you know...

Pizza Hut's changing... with **7 new pizzas** we're raising the taste factor. So if you **love** roasted capsicum, olives & baby spinach try our **new** italian chicken or italian veg

...which will **you** try?

In 2009, Pizza Huts in Australia and New Zealand began using the "Hot Spot" to ensure hot pizza upon delivery. The small black-dot sticker is printed with leuco dyes, which become transparent when they reach a predetermined temperature (+/−5 degrees Celcius). Pizza Hut tuned their dots to disappear at approximately 50 degrees Celcius, or 122 degrees Fahrenheit, revealing the word "HOT" printed with standard ink below. This relatively low temperature outside the box translates to a much higher 68 degrees Celcius, or 155 degrees Fahrenheit, on the inside.

If a customer receives a pizza box that does not show "HOT" on the sticker, she is entitled to a free pizza. This creates an incentive for operators to maintain a high speed of service, because the stores themselves, rather than Pizza Hut corporate, are responsible for paying for the free pizzas.

The box has no ventilation beyond the small tab along the lid's forward edge, so minimal heat is lost due to steam release. Unfortunately, the Hot Spot sticker cannot be placed inside the box and is therefore subject only to temperature fluctuation outside the highly insulated container.

INTERNATIONAL

Domino's Pizza famously changed its recipe in 2009, launching a huge campaign in the media and on their pizza boxes. This Turkish box boasts about a new "peerless sauce . . . We've used plenty of it on all of our pizzas . . . We've brought our flavor to its peak. Is that enough for you?"

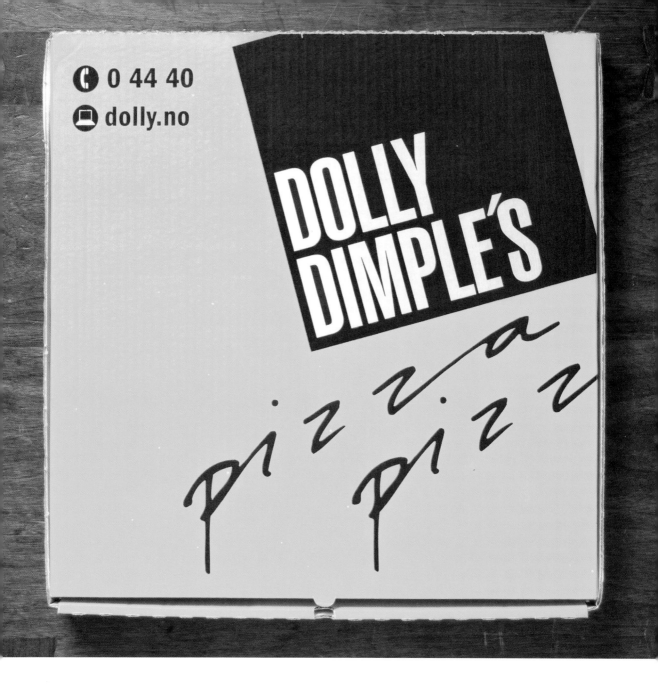

Norwegians eat more pizza per capita than residents of any other country. Dolly Dimple's is the country's second largest pizza company.

Gusto e Tradizione

la Schiacciata

Schiacciata is a double-crusted pizza with fillings in the center and a likely influence on the stuffed pizzas of Chicago. This box comes from Catania, Italy, where the dish is common. The phrase on the box translates to "Taste and Tradition," and the term *schiacciata* also refers to a slam dunk in basketball.

PIZZA
Made in Sicily

At the center, we see a pizza trimmed into the shape of Sicily, surrounded by a ring of Sicilian imagery. Eggplants (*melanzane*) and citrus are both common in Sicily, and the three-legged figure, known as the *triskelion*, is the symbol of the island.

This French stock box contains the post-bake proud chef motif (see pages 82–83) with a bizarre beachfront scene out the window.

heiss & fetzig

PIZZA Pimps

☆ Pimp
☆ Chessy
☆ Light

☆ Bacon Pizza
☆ Classic Italia
☆ Country Pizza
☆ Curry Pizza
☆ CurryPorree
☆ De Mare
☆ Flug Pizza
☆ Garnella

☆ Gyros Pizza
☆ Gorgonzola Pizza
☆ Halloumi Pizza
☆ Hawai
☆ Käse Pizza
☆ Lachs Spinat Pizza
☆ Männer Pizza
☆ Mista

☆ Parma Pizza
☆ Parmazola
☆ Ruccola Pizza
☆ Rustikal Pizza
☆ Summer
☆ Salami Pizza
☆ Sardellen Pizza

☆ Scampi
☆ Spaghetti
☆ Tonno
☆ Vegetaria
☆ Extra Zutaten
_____

An unorthodox menu accompanies this German pizzeria's custom box. "Heiss & fetzig" translates to "Hot & crazy."

Join us on
Facebook
www.facebook.com/pizzapoint

www.pizzapoint.com.pk

PIZZA POINT

taste the perfection!

Pizza Point offers tonnes of premium pizza choices to satisfy every taste bud...

24x7 Free Delivery

All Karachi FREE Delivery **24** Hours

VISA   MasterCard

Accepted

Karachi, Pakistan

CAFETERÍA
el rincón del CINE

MONUMENTO NACIONAL · 1998
HOTEL NACIONAL
de Cuba
★★★★★

Telf: 836 3564 ext. 133, 138 y 795

CAFETERÍA

SERVICIO
24 HORAS

Sydney, Australia

▲ Basel, Switzerland

▲ Various locations, Austria

American pizza boxes usually reference Italy as a way to claim some level of authenticity, but most of the world was oblivious to the dish before it gained popularity in the United States after World War II. These boxes pay homage to America with images that have nothing to do with the food itself. Uncle Sam, lasso-toting cowboys, and the world's largest burger chain provide inspiration for these three boxes.

▶ This custom box from a fast-food shop in Kazakhstan stresses its policy of being open "7/24" with the phrase "We work without days off!"

7/24
Работаем
без выходных!

PIZZA

Mc Burger

Пр-т Абылай хана, 60, уг. ул. Макатаева
тел.: 273-90-97
ТЦ "Рамстор" мкр-н Самал 2
ТД "Люмир", 1 этаж

Производство ТОО "Эмин LTD" (727)3820022, (727)3820025

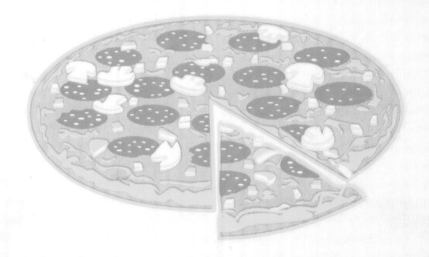

פיצה מושחרת

Here are two boxes from Israel. ▲ This generic pizza box features Israel's version of the proud chef motif (see pages 82–83). The Hebrew block lettering at the top means "worldwide pizza," and Hebrew script at the bottom provide typical phrases "Bon appétit" and "Always hot and tasty." ◀ The phrase on this box translates to "chosen pizza."

Various locations, China

Taipei, Taiwan

Tokyo, Japan

Japan. The sticker here reads "Please eat no later than midnight."

Pizza

Debrecen, Hungary

Prague, Czech Republic

Various locations, Czech Republic

Warsaw, Poland

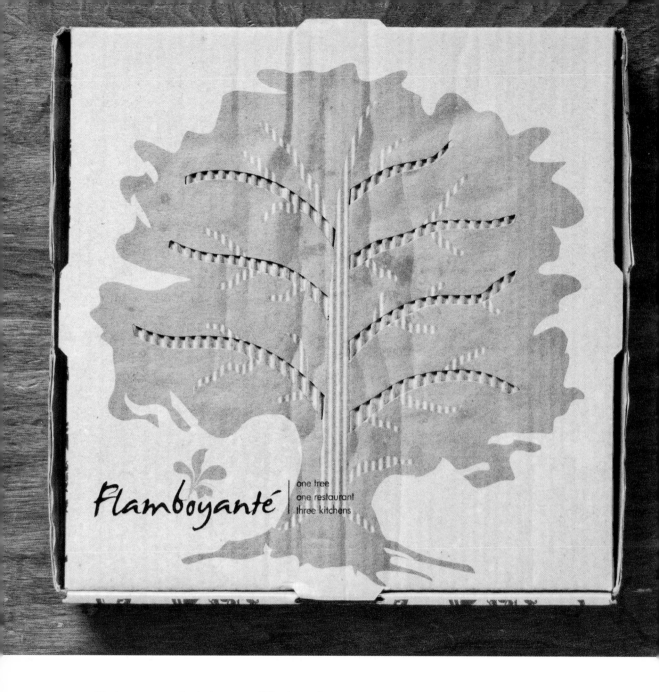

The large tree growing in the center of Flamboyanté's
central dining room in Mumbai is so iconic that it has
become the central image on their pizza box.

London's Pizza Express has cleverly integrated ventilation into their box design in an effort to release steam without distracting the eye from their logo.

Stock box, Liechtenstein

Various locations, Ecuador

Because of New York City's position as one of the world's greatest pizza destinations, its skyline has become a popular image on the boxes and menus of pizzerias around the planet. This stock box from the Brooklyn distributor Joseph Campagna & Sons is the first to depict the post-9/11 skyline featuring the "Freedom Tower" at 1 World Trade Center.

The blue smudge along the bottom of the flag and halos around the buildings are indicative of heavy print pressure on the dense paperboard substrate.

Following the events of September 11, 2001, several companies printed American flags on their boxes. The first to do so was likely Freeport Paper in Central Islip, Long Island, which ran their first batch on September 18, 2001, after an office manager noticed the shortage of flags in nearby stores. People cut the flag out of their used pizza boxes and displayed them in place of the real thing.

ACKNOWLEDGMENTS

This book would have been impossible without the friends, family, pizza tour customers, and complete strangers who shipped me pizza boxes from all corners of the planet. The Turner family, Yuriy Portnikov, Eric Collins, Jeff Randolph, Barbara Gross, Aibek Iskakov, Kate Thomas, Petr Kotasek, Shirley Chow (www.photos-ofpizzaboxes.com), Shauna Sibbald, Katie McClenahan, Mike Beeby, Stefan Pühringer, Greg and Dylan Dollak, Jasper Beekmans, Joey Campagna, Joseph Riggio, Hiroki Kimura, Per Christiansen, Eddie Abe, Renée Teernstra, Rachel Cohn, Luca Ciancio, Tina Foster, Ben Cumming at Hell Pizza, Patrick and Kristy Filler, Jared Lander, Omar Quadir, Kenny Dunn, Pagliacci's Pizza, Mike Madan, Celita Diaz-Perillo, Jeff Randolph, Joshua Barer, Rana Ayhan, Robb and Elissa Alvey, John Correll, John Arena, Ed Hardy, Joel Alter, Nick Sherman, and Tom Monaghan all provided additional assistance in researching and collecting boxes for this book.

Special thanks to the pizza box manufacturers who invited me to their facilities and endured thousands of phone calls and e-mails from me. Thanks to Claudia Gandini and Michael Hoskins at RockTenn for their early support of this book. Special thanks to Manuel Santos for helping me pillage the storage closets at RockTenn's facility in Wakefield, Massachusetts. Thanks to Bob Reid for showing me the Staten Island mill at Pratt Industries. Huge thanks to Diego Rubino at INPACT for helping me dissect his high-tech pizza box and for chauffeuring me around the wonderful city of Naples, Italy. Thanks to Hal Porter and Charlie Kidd for showing me around the stockroom at the Star Pizza Boxes facility in Lakeland, Florida. Thanks to Mike Clark at Stronghaven Containers for a fantastic conversation about corrugation at the 2013 International Pizza Expo in Las Vegas. Thanks to Gil Korine and the entire crew at Freeport Paper for their excitement and for helping me trace the history of pizza box printing. Thanks to Pat Trilli for sharing his wonderful recollections of selling pizza boxes in the 1950s.

Thanks to the entire crew at Melville House, particularly Dennis Johnson for saving an exciting pizza box ten years ago. Thanks to Kelly Burdick for guiding the project brilliantly and to Christopher King for giving the boxes life with his fantastic photography.

Thanks to my dad for teaching me how to tie up the recycling and to my mom for e-mailing me photos of boxes just in case I didn't yet have them. Thanks to Dan and Alicia for lugging back an amazing box from Belgium. Thanks to Jon for the incredible engineering of the purchase, transportation, and storage of the largest commercially available pizza on Earth. And to Renée for putting up with—and dare I say encouraging—my collection of other peoples' garbage and the rerouting of multiple vacations to visit pizza box facilities.

My most sincere apologies to anyone I may have missed and to all the boxes that didn't make it into the book. If you find an amazing pizza box, please get in touch and send it over.

The background for most pizza box photos is a table from Famous Original Ray's on Ninth Ave and Twenty-Third Street in New York City. Special thanks to Agatha Mangano for giving me the table.

IMAGE CREDITS

8 Domino's Pizza box photographed with permission of Tom Monaghan / 9 Photo by Michael Berman (msbphotography.com) / 14 Photo courtesy of Getty Images / 22 "Donna's Pizza" by Donna's Pizza; "Margherita Pizza Inc." by Margherita Pizza Inc. / 23 Box by Ray's Restaurant / 24 "Pacman Pie" by Cheney Brothers / 25 "Phrases" by Savona-Stavola / 26 "Made from the finest ingredients" by RockTenn / 27 "Pizza Bag" by Fischer Paper Products, Inc. / 28 "Sam's Restaurant & Pizzeria" by Sam's Restaurant / 30 "Sal's" by Star Pizza Boxes / 31 "You've Tried All the Rest, Now Try the Best!" by Converted Paper / 32 "Fresh-Hot-Delicious" by Pratt Industries; "Repeating Pizza Men" by Converted Paper / 33 "It's the Greatest!" by Midvale Paper Box Company, Inc. / 35 "Ernie's Pizzeria" by Ernie's Pizza / 38 "Café" by Roma Foods; "Café" by RockTenn / 39 "Pizzeria" by Star Pizza Boxes / 40 LEFT TO RIGHT, FROM TOP: "Street Scene" by CM Design; "Courtyard" by Ferraro Foods; "Buon Appetito!" by DeStefano Foods Inc. / 41 "Dinner for Two" by RockTenn / 43 "Pizza Town" by Tamikee Jennings for Ferraro Foods / 44 "Italian Village" by RockTenn / 45 "Street Scene" by Whalen Packaging / 47 "Picasso's" by Michael Biondo for Picasso's Pizza / 48 "Red Brick" by Star Pizza Boxes / 49 "Sorrento" by Star Pizza Boxes; "Enjoy your delicious moments!" by Jetro/Restaurant Depot / 50–51 "Café" by Holly Del Re for Freeport Paper / 51 "Business Card" by Pasquale Trilli for Converted Paper / 52 "Pizza Picnic" by Migro Catering (Italy) / 53 "Pizza Bay" by SIFA / 54–55 "Tour of Italy: Florence" and "Tour of Italy: Venice" by Roma Foods / 56 "Harvest" by RockTenn / 57 "Season's Greetings" by RockTenn / 58 "Pizza by the Bay" by RockTenn for Costas Provisions / 59 "Rolling Hills" by RockTenn for Sysco / 60 "Christmas" and "Football" by Roma Foods / 61 "Cupid" by Roma Foods / 62–63 "Naples To-Go" and "Naples Pizzaiolo" by Luca Ciancio (Italy) / 66–67 "Farinella" by Farinella Bakery / 68 "Pizza Pizza Pizza" by INPACT (Italy) / 69 "Pizzanista" by Pizzanista / 70 "Tony's Pizza Napoletana" by Ed Hardy for Tony's Pizza Napoletana / 72 "La Hacienda—Fiftieth Anniversary" by La Hacienda / 73 "Tony Boloney's" by Michael Hauke for Tony Boloney's / 74 "Giordano's" by Giordano's / 75 "Picasso's" by Larry Santora for Picasso's / 76 "Pizzatown, U.S.A." by Pizzatown, U.S.A / 77 "Regina" by Regina Pizzeria / 78 "La Perla" by La Perla (The Netherlands) / 79 "Joseph's" by Joseph's Pizza / 82 "Proud Chef," both by Toscana Ondulati / 83 "Two-Color Chef" by Master Packaging / 85 "Bandanna" by Liner Italia International / 87–91 "Joyride," "Serenade," "Pizza Babe," "Totò e Troisi," "Totò e Peppino," and "Totò e Sophia Loren" by Luca Ciancio / 92 "Tony's Pizza Toss" by Star Pizza Boxes for Tony's New York Pizza / 93 "Pizza Toss" by Liner Italia / 98 "Table Box" by Tabletop Pizza Box / 100–101 "GreenBox" by William Walsh, Ecovention, LLC / 102–103 "Hell Pizza" by Hell Pizza (New Zealand) / 104–105 "Green Monster" by Papa Gino's Pizza / 106 "Puzzle" by PackToy, PHD Business / 107 "Connect 4x4" by Hasbro Gaming for Domino's / 108 "Hatsune Miku" by Domino's Japan / 110–111 "Rossopomodoro" by INPACT for Rossopomodoro/Eataly / 112 "Juno's Pizza" by Shree Krishna Packaging for Juno's Pizza / 113 "CPK," both by Shree Krishna Packaging for California Pizza Kitchen / 114–115 "Hot Spot" by Pizza Hut / 118 "Is That Enough for You?" by Domino's Turkey / 119 "Dolly Dimple's" by Dolly Dimple's / 123 "Pizza Pimps" by Pizza Pimps / 124 "Pizza Point" by Pizza Point / 125 "El Rincón Cine" by El Rincón Cine / 126 "Bushman" by Australia's Pizza House / 128 "Sam's Pizza Land" by Sam's Pizza Land; "Western Weeks" by Pizza Mann / 129 "McBurger" by McBurger / 132 LEFT TO RIGHT, FROM TOP: "Pizza 2 Pizza" by Pizza 2 Pizza; "Caf'e Grazie" by Café Grazie; "Frey's Famous Pizzeria" by Frey's Famous Pizzeria / 133 "Pizza Pizza" by Pizza Yanee / 135 LEFT TO RIGHT, FROM TOP: "Pizza Vespa" by Pizza Vespa; "Pizzeria Pavaon" by Pizzeria Pavaon; "Gar" by Gar Ristorante / 136 "VENTiT Tree" by Flamboyanté / 137 "Pizza Express" by Pizza Express / 138 "Mangiamos" by Mangiamos / 139 "Pizzeria el Hornero" by Pizzeria el Hornero / 141 "Freedom Tower" by Joseph Campagna & Sons / Every effort has been made to contact copyright holders of pictures used in this book. If you are the copyright holder of any uncredited image herein, please contact the publisher.

ABOUT THE AUTHOR

SCOTT WIENER'S writing appears online at Serious Eats and on his blog, Scott's Pizza Journal. His award-winning column, "Man on the Street," appears monthly in *Pizza Today Magazine*. He is the founder of Scott's Pizza Tours, which guides tourists and New Yorkers though the history, science, and culture of New York City pizza (www.scottspizzatours.com). The tours have been featured on the Food Network, the Cooking Channel, the Travel Channel, the Discovery Channel, Lonely Planet, and a host of other outlets. Wiener maintains the world's largest archive of unique pizza boxes.